SYMPHONY NO. 1
IN G MINOR

RECENT RESEARCHES IN THE MUSIC OF THE NINETEENTH
AND EARLY TWENTIETH CENTURIES

Rufus Hallmark, general editor

A-R Editions, Inc., publishes six quarterly series—

Recent Researches in the Music of the Middle Ages and Early Renaissance
Margaret Bent, general editor

Recent Researches in the Music of the Renaissance
James Haar, general editor

Recent Researches in the Music of the Baroque Era
Robert L. Marshall, general editor

Recent Researches in the Music of the Classical Era
Eugene K. Wolf, general editor

Recent Researches in the Music of the Nineteenth and Early Twentieth Centuries
Rufus Hallmark, general editor

Recent Researches in American Music
H. Wiley Hitchcock, general editor—

which make public music that is being brought to light
in the course of current musicological research.

Each volume in the *Recent Researches* is devoted
to works by a single composer or to a single genre of composition,
chosen because of its potential interest to scholars and performers,
and prepared for publication according to the standards that govern
the making of all reliable historical editions.

Subscribers to this series, as well as patrons of subscribing institutions,
are invited to apply for information about the "Copyright-Sharing Policy"
of A-R Editions, Inc., under which the contents of this volume
may be reproduced free of charge for study or performance.

Correspondence should be addressed:

A-R EDITIONS, INC.
315 West Gorham Street
Madison, Wisconsin 53703

RECENT RESEARCHES IN THE MUSIC OF THE NINETEENTH
AND EARLY TWENTIETH CENTURIES • VOLUME VI

Etienne-Nicolas Méhul

SYMPHONY NO. 1 IN G MINOR

Edited by David Charlton

A-R EDITIONS, INC. • MADISON

All inquires regarding performance and recording rights should be addressed to the publisher.

Performance parts are available from the publisher.

© 1985 by A-R Editions, Inc.
All rights reserved
Printed in the United States of America

Library of Congress Cataloging in Publication Data:

Méhul, Étienne Nicolas, 1763–1817.
   [Symphonies, no. 1, G minor]
   Symphony no. 1 in G minor.

   (Recent researches in the music of the nineteenth and early twentieth centuries, ISSN 0193–5364 ; v. 6)
   Includes historical information, editorial procedures, and bibliographical references.
   1. Symphonies—Scores.   I. Charlton, David, 1946–
II. Series.
M2.R23834   vol. 6   [M1001]   84-758050
ISBN 0-89579-174-9

Contents

Preface	vii
The Composer	vii
Parisian Concert Life Leading into the Napoleonic Era	vii
Méhul the Symphonist	viii
Symphony No. 1 in G Minor	x
Performance Practice	xii
The Sources	xiii
Editorial Principles	xiv
Critical Notes	xv
Acknowledgments	xvi
Notes	xvii
Plate I	xix
Plate II	xx
Plate III	xxi
Symphony No. 1 in G Minor	
Allegro	1
Andante	31
Menuet. Allegro moderato	54
Final. Allegro agitato	65
Appendix 1	103
Appendix 2	104

Preface

Fétis described Méhul in 1830 as "one of the greatest musicians that France has produced," but Méhul's considerable symphonic achievements are only now coming to be fully understood. His Symphony No. 1 in G Minor (1808–1809) is a remarkable and inspired example of art from the "age of Beethoven," and a landmark in the history of the French symphony. The work has not been published in score since the first edition prepared under Méhul's supervision.

The Composer

Etienne-Nicolas Méhul was born at Givet, northern France, on 22 June 1763, and died in Paris from pulmonary consumption on 18 October 1817. Under the Revolution and Empire he was to become, with Cherubini, France's most important composer, and a figure whose name and works were known throughout the musical western world. Méhul was certainly ambitious, but he was also a more generous person than some were later to claim. "All those who knew Méhul more closely, know that there are few about whom more honorable facts could be cited."[1]

Méhul came to Paris in 1778 or 1779, thereafter completing his musical apprenticeship under J. F. Edelmann. He published six youthful keyboard sonatas, and his vocal music was heard at the Concert Spirituel as early as 1782.[2]

In the 1790s, Méhul's name became a byword for all that was original, dramatic, and modern in the field of opéra-comique. His command of serious drama (opéra-comique by now embracing the whole range of subject-matter) and of innovative orchestration, as well as his teaching and inspectoral roles at the new Paris Conservatoire, all contributed to his uniquely authoritative position. From opéras-comiques such as *Euphrosine, Stratonice, Mélidore et Phrosine,* and *Ariodant* (1790–1799), with their almost consistent concern with jealousy and sexual repression, Méhul turned eventually to write comic scores such as *L'irato, Une folie,* and *Les deux aveugles de Tolède* (1801–1806); these were more widely appreciated than the earlier dramas had been.[3] And, although his most famous opéra-comique *Joseph* (1807) was not a particular success in contemporary Paris, it became known in theaters everywhere for much of the nineteenth century, epitomizing the Romantic religiosity that had prompted its creation.

Already in 1797 (see below) Méhul had a symphony performed with some success; it does not, however, survive in complete form. His interest in orchestral music *per se* was thereafter pursued in several opéra-comique overtures; in fact, the first movement of his future Symphony No. 2 in D (1809) started life as an overture, albeit with a main Allegro different to the one familiar today.[4] At least two catalysts were at work preceding the burst of activity from 1808 to 1810 that saw the composition of the five numbered Méhul symphonies: first, the composer's disillusionment with stage composition, and second, the impetus provided by symphonies of Haydn, Mozart, and Beethoven. The disillusionment was noted in a letter whose text survives in summarized form: "Tired of the aggravations of the theater, he wished to attempt a completely independent genre of composition."[5] The impetus provided by the Viennese compositions is best seen against the background of Parisian concert life at the time.

Parisian Concert Life
Leading into the Napoleonic Era

The importance and extent of the contribution of French composers to the eighteenth-century symphony has been charted in detail in Barry S. Brook's magisterial study, *La symphonie française*.[6] At least 110 symphonies by French composers are known from the period 1778 to 1789, for example. The main contributors were Henri-Joseph Rigel (1741–1799), who published seven symphonies (one in G minor); Louis-Charles Ragué (before 1760–after 1793) and Marie-Alexandre Guénin (1744–1835), each of whom published three symphonies in 1787–88; and François-Joseph Gossec (1734–1829), the recognized leader of the French symphonic school.

However, if one takes performance patterns at the Concert Spirituel in the 1780s as a guide to Parisian taste, a lessening of interest in "French" symphonies is perceptible. After three performances in 1782, Gossec's symphonies were heard only twice more in these famous concerts. The number of French symphonists represented in performance dropped from six in 1781 (Gossec, Rigel, Simon Leduc, Nicolas Capron, Louis de Froment, and "De Beket" (Franz Beck?)) to one in 1789 (Pierre-Joseph Candeille, 1744–1827). But during the same period the five performances of Haydn's symphonies that took place in 1781 grew to twenty-six in 1786 and to thirty-five in 1789.[7] Meanwhile, at the Concerts de la Loge Olympique, Haydn's "Paris" symphonies, Nos. 82 to 87, were receiving their premieres in 1787.

With one exception, no symphonies by native Frenchmen survive from the years 1790 to 1807; this exception is J. B. Bédard's *No. 1 Simphonie périodique* (ca. 1800).[8] A handful of works by Guénin, Louis Jadin, and others were produced but, until rediscovered, cannot be assessed. Most serious Parisian composition was intended for opera and opéra-comique, though large numbers of surviving concertos, overtures, symphonies concertantes, and so on were written as well. The more prolific instrumental composers were Jean-Baptiste Bréval, François Devienne, Rodolphe Kreutzer, and Louis Jadin; of these, Devienne and Kreutzer also wrote successful opéras-comiques. On the other hand, opéra-comique composers such as Méhul, Luigi Cherubini, Nicolas Dalayrac, and Henri-Montan Berton tended to avoid writing display pieces or chamber music. The outstanding representatives of the rising generation, Charles-Simon Catel and Adrien Boieldieu, tended towards the operatic path. A third group of composers were those virtuosos specializing in music for their instrument: Viotti and Rode (violin), Frédéric Blasius, J. X. Lefèvre, and Etienne Ozi (woodwind), and Victor Duvernoy (horn).

Concert life in Paris was disrupted to some extent by the cessation of the Concert Spirituel in February or April 1790,[9] but many new musical events arose to fill its place, and not simply during Lent. In particular, the orchestra of the Théâtre Feydeau was celebrated (this is the theater first called the Théâtre de Monsieur on its foundation in 1789). Viotti directed it, prior to his emigration to London. This ensemble gave first performances of French instrumental works in 1792–1794 and so steadfast was its fashionable clientèle that in December 1794, only five months after the fall of Robespierre, women in the audience attracted adverse press comment by wearing silk clothes.[10] The Feydeau orchestra played Méhul's early unnumbered symphony in 1797. Other ensembles gave concerts, often on state occasions, and some of these were organized by the Institut national de musique, forerunner of the Paris Conservatoire.

Newly founded concert organizations under the Directory and Consulate (1795–1804) included the Conservatoire pupils' concerts (called *Exercices*); the Concerts de la rue de Cléry (founded 1798–99); and the Concerts rue Grenelle (founded 1803).[11] The Conservatoire concerts, springing in 1800 from a tradition of annual prizegiving concerts, numbered between five and twelve each season. Their program-building, supervised eventually by Méhul and Cherubini, was as valued as were their performance standards, at least among those music-lovers who valued quality and eclecticism above virtuosity and fashion. Until the new Conservatoire concert-hall was opened in 1811, the concerts were held in the cramped conditions of an auditorium originally used for opéra-comique.[12] A report from 1810 reveals their special atmosphere:

> The first concert took place on Sunday 18 February, and all the old *habitués* found themselves reunited in the too-narrow precinct given over to the concerts long before the doors were even opened. These concerts, independently of their rare merit, have a particular charm in the composition of the audience; almost always the same seat and same neighbors, the same way of listening, feeling, and understanding, just as the same method in the performers. All in this little space seems in harmony with taste and affection. Electricity in its movement has no more rapidity than the sensation communicated to such an audience by a phrase of musical genius, or of perfect execution.[13]

In time the orchestra built up a nucleus of excellent players attached to the Conservatoire teaching staff. Several reports in the *Allgemeine musikalische Zeitung* informed German readers of the merits of these *exercices*.[14]

Following on the above-mentioned popularity of Haydn's music in the 1780s, Mozart's music, too, enjoyed a good reception in Paris, particularly after 1800. Not only were the *Mystères d'Isis* (*Die Zauberflöte* adapted) and the Requiem successfully given in 1801 and 1804, respectively, but J.F. Rochlitz's eulogistic book, *Anecdotes sur W. G.* [sic] *Mozart*, which referred to his "Shakespearian" genius, appeared in 1801. Between 1805 and 1808 the six "Haydn" quartets (K. V. 387, 417b (421), 458, 421b (438), 464, and 465) were issued by a French publisher;[15] and J. J. de Momigny's analysis of his D minor string quartet K. V. 417b appeared in 1806.[16] At the Conservatoire concerts, isolated pieces drawn from Mozart's operas were performed from 1803, but suddenly in 1807 there were also four performances of Mozart overtures and six of his symphonies, including one in G minor on 26 April.[17] Méhul's approval, if not his personal program design, can be assumed. One of his surviving autograph pages of notes records his admiration for Mozart's "profusion of effects" and "richness of style."[18]

Equally or more significant in this gestation period for Méhul's mature symphonies were the Conservatoire performances of Beethoven's First Symphony on 22 February 1807 and 10 April 1808. In their pioneering work on Méhul's symphonies, Boris Schwarz and Alexander Ringer drew attention to the evidence of François Habeneck, who was later celebrated as the founding musical director (in 1828) of the Société des Concerts du Conservatoire but was already a trusted graduate student conductor under the First Empire. Habeneck told Anton Schindler in winter 1840/41 that Beethoven's first two symphonies had been the immediate stimulus behind the composition of Méhul's own. Méhul had witnessed Habeneck rehearsing these works with a chamber orchestra some time before their public appearance in Paris.[19] Indeed there are obvious parallels between the opening allegros of Beethoven's and Méhul's second symphonies, both in D.

Méhul the Symphonist

We may now proceed to a chronological account of the six known symphonies by Méhul. They comprise a partially extant symphony in C, not given a number by the composer, and performed in 1797; No. 1, G Minor (the work in the present edition); No. 2, D Major (modern score issued in 1957 by Editions Musicales Transatlantiques, ed. F. Oubradous); No. 3, C Major; No. 4, E Major; and No. 5, A Major (incomplete). (The last three symphonies, discovered by the present editor, were first published by Garland Publishing (New York, London, 1982): *Etienne-Nicolas Méhul 1763–1817 Three Symphonies,* volume 8 of Series D of The Symphony 1720–1840, under the general editorship of Barry S. Brook.)

Symphony "0" (1797)

The direct evidence for this work is found in press announcements and reviews. It was played on 28 January and on 7 February at the seventh and eighth concerts given by the Théâtre Feydeau orchestra. The first reviewer did not give specific details such as the piece's tonality (this type of casual reporting was all too common) but declared "the second part of the concert began with a charming symphony by M. Méhul; we recognize in it all the talent of this skillful composer."[20] The autograph score probably corresponding to this work is Bibliothèque Nationale MS 2271 (4, 5); all that remains is an Andante in F and a Presto in C. Haydn's influence is paramount, both in the formal character of the music and in its thematic substance, though the piece is more than just competently handled.

(The "Symphony in C" mistakenly claimed for Méhul by Constant Pierre and played at the Conservatoire concert of 30 January 1802 was actually by Haydn, according to the newspaper sources cited by Pierre himself.[21] The so-called "Symphony" that Edouard Gregoir noticed as announced for 12 and 23 January 1806 must, in fact, have been one of Méhul's overtures. It was given in a ballroom at 10:00 P.M., in a series in which Méhul's popular *La chasse du jeune Henri* overture had previously been featured.)[22]

Symphony No. 1 in G Minor

Once again we have no direct evidence outside the press for establishing a date of first performance. But the circumstantial evidence suggests that Méhul had two, or even three, symphonies ready for performance in 1808, one of which was the G minor. On Thursday 3 November that year, a "manuscript symphony by M. Méhul" was given at the opening concert of the Cercle Musical de la cour Mandar, under the direction of "M. Lefèvre."[23] In the company of "a great number of composers and artists of the first merit," the new symphony "was overwhelmed with applause, and was found most beautiful, even when heard after one of the most magnificent symphonies of Haydn." The same report noted the presence of the composers Berton, Nicolo [Nicolas Isouard], and Reichard [Johann Friedrich Reichardt] at the concert. No Méhul work was noticed in the review of the second Mandar concert, which presumably took place on Thursday 17 November.[24] But the reviewer added:

> A new symphony by M. Méhul has been announced for the next concert. This is to promise us an assured pleasure. This famous composer, pursuing in a glorious manner the path revealed by Haydn and Mozart, can only spread a new brilliance over the French school, of which he is one of the worthiest mainstays.

Unfortunately, no report of the third Mandar concert, which presumably took place on Thursday 1 December, has been found in the press. However, an undated autograph letter by Méhul to his friend, the composer Berton, allows us to deduce that another symphony by him was, indeed, played at the third Mandar concert.

> My dear Berton, I counted on having the pleasure of seeing you this morning, but the weather is so bad, the fireside corner is so good, it is so easy to chat with pen in hand and slippers on one's feet that I write thus, first, to thank you for having thought of my symphony for Thursday's concert and to tell you that, after much reflection, I have found some jeopardy in giving a first performance at a great display concert where they come primarily to be seen, next to hear Rode [the celebrated violinist], nothing but Rode, and then to criticize as much as possible since, having paid more money than usual, they will also be harder to please. So I shall wait for the ordinary concerts, where they will come for the music, and cheaply; there I can take my chances, and for that I shall entreat your goodwill.
>
> I am sorry that you didn't come to le Febvre's last concert. You would have heard a new symphony that probably would have pleased you more than the first, after which you might have invited Etienne [C.-E. Etienne of the *Journal de l'empire*] to say two words about it, and you know that, for us, two good words printed in a good paper are the sweetest recompense we could receive, after the esteem of true artists. I embrace you. Méhul.
>
> A thousand friendly compliments to Madame Berton.[25]

The symphony which Méhul was here reportedly withdrawing from Lefèvre's (fourth) concert might have been a repeat of one of the earlier two, or, very possibly a new, third work. His reference to "ordinary concerts" is a clear allusion to the Conservatoire *exercices*, whose atmosphere we have described above, and for which the admission fee was only half that of other concerts.[26] In conclusion, nothing permits us to say definitely that the G Minor Symphony was heard under Lefèvre's direction; but the existence of a fragment of an earlier version of this score (see Appendix 2) lends weight to the supposition that the work was in existence in 1808.

The autograph manuscript of the first movement of the G Minor Symphony is entitled "Simphonie No. 1" (see Plate II) and this, we can say with virtual certainty, was the work played at the Conservatoire concert on 12 March 1809. There were three press reviews. The first two appeared after two days. (The third review, *Moniteur universel*, 17 March 1809, pp. 303–304, is reprinted in Pougin, *Méhul*, pp. 300–302.)

> We shall also mention the symphony by M. Méhul, whose superior beauties, performed with a truly admirable *ensemble* and firmness, received every acclaim. If it is true, as we are assured, that this great musician has written three pieces of this merit and importance, such labors must prove epoch-making in a school [i.e., France] where for forty years Haydn's superior talent and great reputation seemed to weigh heavily on all composers, effectively preventing them from writing in this genre, one of the most beautiful and difficult of all in music.[27]
>
> M. Méhul has desired to reconquer for France a branch of music that she had entirely lost. M. Gossec formerly deployed very fine talent in his symphonies; but since Haydn astonished and charmed Europe with his numerous productions, it was given to Mozart alone to be heard with pleasure beside that great master. M. Méhul, without seeking to imitate these two illustrious

composers, abandoned himself to the stimulus of a brilliant imagination and to the resources opened to him by the profound knowledge of his art; finally he found the now rare secret of being novel without appearing bizarre, and of linking the best calculations of harmonic richness to the most beguiling melody. It would take more space than we have here to give details of all parts of the work we have just heard, [or] to give an idea of the skill with which M. Méhul brings together all the instruments (among them the cellos) in ravishing ensemble effect; we shall confine ourselves to announcing that at last we have a *French symphonist,* and that the concert under review was a veritable triumph for him.[28]

Second Symphony

Méhul's Second Symphony, announced and reviewed as such, was then played by the Conservatoire orchestra on 26 March, 2 April, and 23 April 1809.[29] The autograph score (Méhul's only complete symphony autograph to survive) and the printed material show this to be the D Major Symphony. It was evidently the Parisian favorite.

On 21 May 1809 Méhul's Third Symphony was played by the same orchestra. It was reviewed in two newspapers, with considerable warmth. The original manuscript orchestra parts have only recently come to light, permitting the first publication as cited above.

One of the two reviewers of the Third Symphony drew attention to some kind of "opposition party" that was forming against Méhul's new path. Cherubini's *Anacréon* overture, already admired, was bound to be successful at the concert. But, the reviewer continued,

> As for the symphony, success was less certain. That of the first two had been great; but such is the situation of M. Méhul that, in order to defeat the ridiculous prejudice of certain people who seem to wish to prevent any musician from writing symphonies just because Haydn and Mozart wrote admirable ones, he must needs surpass himself with each new production. This is what he has done.[30]

But the audience reaction was what counted, and neither the First nor the Third was repeated. It must have been at this juncture that Méhul wrote to François Sauvo of the *Moniteur universel* to thank him for his interest and reports, and declared:

> Passionate admirer of Haydn's music, I understood all the dangers of my enterprise; I foresaw the cautious welcome that the music-lovers would give my symphonies. . . . I plan to write new ones for next winter, and shall try to write them so as to merit your esteem and to accustom the public gradually to think that a Frenchman may follow Haydn and Mozart at a distance.[31]

Symphony No. 4 in E

On 17 March 1810 Méhul's Symphony No. 4 in E was played at the Conservatoire, in its original version. The piece was in part deliberately evocative of Haydn's style, as a token of homage to the master recently deceased. As mentioned above, the finding of the manuscript orchestra parts has recently permitted the first publication of the work. The four reviews that were published were not in agreement about the merits or demerits of each movement. Subsequently, the composer rewrote his third movement and finale, and the work in its final form shows Méhul still developing in originality of symphonic thought.

Fifth Symphony

The autograph score of Méhul's Fifth Symphony consists only of a slow introduction and an Allegro first movement, in A major. It perhaps dates from late 1810 or 1811.[32] It is not known to have been performed and has, with Symphonies Three and Four, only recently been published. But a contemporaneous performance may have been planned by Méhul, since in Choron and Fayolle's *Dictionnaire historique des musiciens* (Paris, 1810–1811) the article on this composer mentions "six symphonies which have been successfully performed at the Conservatoire of Music."

Symphony No. 1 in G Minor

After its 1809 performance, Méhul's G Minor Symphony, together with No. 2 in D, was published in Paris in score and in parts (see The Sources below). However, we do not yet know the date of any subsequent nineteenth-century performances in Paris. When the "Catalogue de la musique à l'usage des exercices" was drawn up under the Restoration (between 1815 and 1821) for the internal use of the Conservatoire's successor, the Ecole Royale de Musique et de Déclamation, no Méhul symphony was included, even though symphonies by Gossec, Rigel and Guénin appeared in it beside those of Haydn and Mozart.[33] But that at least one performance of the G Minor Symphony did take place after 1815 we deduce from the present state of the manuscript orchestra parts; some new partbooks were specially copied, incorporating direct cuts that were simultaneously indicated in the older partbooks using *collettes* made from Bourbon government pro-formas.

The attitude of Cherubini towards Méhul's symphonies was so negative that in his life-and-works notes made after his friend's death, he simply classified them together with ballet music, cantatas "and other ephemeral pieces."[34] Over a decade later the same lack of appreciation was maintained by F. J. Fétis. When a Méhul memorial concert was announced for 7 March 1830 at the Ecole Royale de Musique, Fétis wrote in his journal:

> We cannot but applaud the decision that was taken to forgo the performance of a symphony by Méhul. Nature had not organized this great master to treat this genre of music successfully. Seized by the beauties of Haydn's symphonies, he wished to write some in the same system, and while certainly wanting to be rich in developments, he was only dry and pretentious. His genius had been created for the dramatic style.[35]

The same opinion naturally informed Fétis's biography of Méhul, which first appeared in the *Revue musicale* on 20 March 1830 and was perpetuated in his influential *Biographie universelle des musiciens* for the remainder of the century. Not until 8 December 1901 was the G Minor Symphony played at the Société des Concerts du Conservatoire, Paris.[36]

Very different reactions to this work were manifest in Germany and in England. The Leipzig Gewandhaus orchestra played one of the Méhul symphonies on 13 May 1810; neither the official record nor the press review conclusively identified the work, however.[37] In October of that year the publication of the G Minor Symphony by Breitkopf & Härtel was announced,[38] and on 22 November 1810 the piece was played at the Gewandhaus under J. P. C. Schulz. The reviewer of the performance wrote:

> New symphony by Méhul, in G minor. It is certainly not unworthy of this original, artistically experienced, and learned master, but it is unlikely to be very successful in Germany. It is not sufficiently melodic, has too much rushing, artifice, and strangeness. He who sets out to astonish and surprise almost never succeeds. However, we overlook neither the cleverness of invention of many passages nor the industry and extraordinary constructive power in the working-out. Yet, in the latter we fail to find that which alone proves mastery in this field, and through which the achievement of significant effect is assured: patience, perseverance—as it were a fixing in fire, in order to fuse together the happy discoveries into great, pure, solid masses. The very long Andante, tiring and monotonous notwithstanding its constantly changing figures, pleased us least [it was probably played too slowly; see Performance Practice below]; the Finale—which indeed rushed along with unbroken storm and stress, but is at the same time worked out ingeniously and with great variety—pleased us most.[39]

On 1 March 1838 Felix Mendelssohn conducted the G Minor Symphony with the same orchestra. The *Allgemeine musikalische Zeitung* reviews are too lengthy to quote,[40] but Robert Schumann's reaction should be particularly noted, as he found the work "most interesting" and continued,

> it appears to us so different from the German symphonic manner, and at the same time thorough and ingenious, even if somewhat mannered, that we cannot recommend it too highly to foreign [i.e., non-French] orchestras. A remarkable feature, too, was the similarity of the last movement to the first of Beethoven's C minor symphony, and of the scherzos of the same two symphonies, and this in such a striking way that there must have been a remembrance at work on one side or the other; I am not able to determine on which, since I do not know the year of birth of the Méhul [symphony].[41]

As Beethoven's Fifth Symphony was begun in 1805, but only performed on 22 December 1808, there was creative reminiscence neither on his nor on Méhul's part. It is, however, worth recalling that Beethoven could hardly have avoided Méhul's opéras-comiques in Vienna, and that as late as 1823 Beethoven requested scores of Méhul's music from Paris and remarked on the regrettable loss caused by his death.[42]

Support for Méhul's G Minor Symphony was expressed in England well before its first documented public hearing in 1862. The neglect of certain works by the Philharmonic Society was countered in 1843 with the words, "Let us have the symphony in G minor of Méhul, so undeservedly forgotten."[43] In winter 1855/56 Charles Hallé copied out part of the work, but seems not to have conducted it.[44] The work was finally directed by August Manns at a Crystal Palace Saturday Concert on 8 March 1862, announced in *The Times* of that day as "first time of performance in England." The main concert review was historical rather than critical in tone, but ended:

> and it is to be hoped that, emboldened by the real interest with which it was listened to, he [Manns] may be induced, not only to repeat this work, but to try another, sooner or later, from the same pen.[45]

The next hearing, however, was to be under the baton of William Sterndale Bennett, at a Philharmonic Society concert at the Hanover Square Rooms on 2 May 1864. This performance was the occasion for a discerning review by J. W. Davison of *The Times*. After a historically based introduction to the piece, Davison's critical remarks began, "A work of unequal merit, it is, nevertheless, one which shows a high aspiration, contains many genuine beauties, and proclaims indisputably the hand of a master," and concluded, "its revival may be pronounced an unqualified success."[46]

Owing to the work's uneven performance history, it is hard to claim that it had any definite influence upon other composers, except probably Ferdinand Hérold (1791–1833). Hérold was Méhul's pupil, and after winning the Prix de Rome he sent back two symphonies from Italy, written in 1813 and 1814. Several features suggest Méhul's inspiration, of which the most distinctive is the use of a pedal point accompanying main thematic statements. This trait is already seen in the Andante of Méhul's G Minor Symphony, then in the finale of his Second Symphony and the first movement of the Fourth Symphony. Hérold uses the technique in the Andante of his First Symphony and in the Rondo of his Second.[47]

The observations of René Brancour and Alexander Ringer surely remain apposite when they suggest that Mendelssohn may have owed Méhul's work a debt in his C minor symphony (op. 11) and his G minor piano concerto.[48] Although Brahms was certainly an admirer of Méhul's *Uthal*, his knowledge of the present symphony is evinced only in a late letter to Clara Schumann, 10 March 1895, where he simply refers to a pleasurable hearing of "orchestral symphonies by Méhul, Bach, and others" at Meiningen.

The G Minor Symphony has a compactness of instrumentation that would seem a musical antithesis to the composer's operas, criticized in the 1790s for their sometimes violent orchestral power. This notion is deceptive in two ways. First, there is evidence that Méhul originally conceived the Symphony with larger instrumentation; second, the rhythmic unity and drive of its first and last movements produces a kind of tension in performance that is totally modern in sensibility.

The evidence concerning instrumentation is contained on the final leaf of Méhul's autograph score (see Plate I and Appendix 2). This leaf contains music for a full brass section, with four horns, two trumpets, and at least one trombone—that is, for the size of brass choir that had been available to Parisian composers at the Opéra-Comique (for example) since 1797.[49] Appendix 2 thus demonstrates (for the first time in print) the coda of the first movement clothed in traditional Méhullic orchestral armour. It would have been perfectly possible for the composer to have retained this instrumentation when arranging the Conservatoire performance in 1809 (see Performance Practice below). Instead he decided upon a pattern of economy, which he followed in all his later symphonies except No. 3, which alone admits trumpets. As a result, the G Minor Symphony gains in value: it does not overstate its case, and the force of its punches benefits from the greater athleticism of its movement.

The opening Allegro at once shows the astonishing nervous energy so essential to the whole symphony. The rhetorical flourish of the opening, though developed later in the movement, is cast aside in favor of the sparer chromatic motif first exposed in measure 16. Its basic rhythm underlies the second subject at measure 59, and its basic shape returns in measure 84. The tight construction incorporates the development of the dotted rhythm in measure 3, and the scalewise outline of the second subject is embryonically present in the bass motif in measure 2 in sixteenth-notes: Méhul himself clarifies this relationship in measures 57–58. In his formal plan the composer creates something happily distinct from that in either of its better-known G minor forerunners, Haydn's Symphony No. 83 and Mozart's No. 40. By reversing the thematic order of the recapitulation Méhul avoids lowering the tension nearer the end but still retains the major mode for the second subject. Another stroke of formal ingenuity was the rejection of any repeat of the exposition. Instead, at measures 110–11, we plunge without warning into the development, and the ground is swept from under our feet as we hear B-flat minor. A possible model for this fluid transition was the last movement of Beethoven's First Symphony, measures 95–96.

In the Romance of his B-flat "Paris" symphony, No. 85, Haydn used the French folk-tune "La gentille et jeune Lisette,"[50] and Méhul uses a version of the traditional French *noël* "Venez, divin Messie" for his own Andante movement.

etc.

This melody, also known to its sixteenth-century words, "Laissez paître vos bêtes," had been used in organ variations by Nicolas-Antoine Lebègue, André Raison, Claude-Bénigne Balbastre, and most recently Jean-Jacques Beauvarlet-Charpentier in 1782.[51] But Méhul's variations contain a complex wealth of other material as well. The initial thematic paragraph is forty-four measures long, containing three statements of the principal idea (mm. 1, 25, 41). There follows a minor-mode variation of similar length, but already Méhul's avoidance of symmetrical structure is seen in the omission of a variant of the material first heard in measure 16; or rather, the composer *develops* a variant of it as the countersubject, starting in measure 57. Thematic variation produces the optimistic theme heard in measure 100 (used extensively in the closing stages of the movement). Dramatic intervention by tutti fanfare-figures at measure 109 bears a close resemblance to that in Beethoven's Ninth Symphony, Adagio, measure 130, not least in the way the new rhythm infects the music that follows. But Méhul does not distinguish clearly between his episodes of dramatic interaction and those of pure variation, and the outlines of his form become subservient to progressive rhythmic diminution. This leads to the climax at measure 205, followed by the first appearance of horns. Méhul cleverly uses the end of the coda to anticipate the theme of the Menuet.

As Schumann had noticed, the soft pizzicato arpeggios of the Menuet bear an uncanny likeness to those at measure 244 of the third movement of Beethoven's Fifth Symphony; indeed, the trio sections of both movements use a unison scalewise motif in eighth-notes. And, like Beethoven, Méhul adds a coda section; horns enter here for the first time. Again, the coda material (mm. 159, 172) makes a transition from the ghostly, unreal world of the Menuet to the reality of the finale.

The Final (horns pitched up to G as in the Menuet instead of B-flat as in the first two movements) presents a picture of somber intensity. The upbeat rhythm, resembling the "Fate" rhythm of Beethoven's Fifth Symphony, pervades the music with a similar relentlessness. The music is cast in unorthodox sonata form; the first subject is restated in D minor at measure 64. The D-minor second subject, so far from lending any relief, merely qualifies the expression to one of pathos, particularly after the extraordinary and impressionistic tutti that precedes it in measures 76 to 86. The all-pervasive rhythm now underlies the second subject (m. 93), which has itself been superbly prepared for by thematic foreshadowings at measures 5, 29 (grace-notes), 30 and their various developments following. After exploring remote keys in the central section, the composer passes back through the tonic at measure 155; but the full implications of his subtle formal scheme are not apparent until measure 220, when the main theme returns in G minor *after* an apparent recapitulation in C minor, but with perfect logic. So Méhul creates a classical yet an individual sonata, enabling him to prolong both the tension and the variety, which intensify to the very end.

Performance Practice

The Ensemble

We do not know the size of the orchestra of the Cercle Musical de la Cour Mandar. As a comparison, the Concerts de la rue de Cléry (founded ca. 1799) had an orchestra of eighty, according to one later writer.[52] More is known about the Conservatoire orchestra. Although it comprised about 60 players in 1802,[53] by 1813–1814 it comprised some 30 violins, 8 violas, 14 cellos, 6 double-basses, pairs of flutes, oboes, and clarinets, 4 bassoons, 4 horns, a timpanist, and 2 trombonists. A trumpeter was brought in as required. About thirty of the players were non-students of professional status.[54] Méhul's G Minor

Symphony was probably played by a similarly sized ensemble in 1809.

Attention should be drawn to Méhul's use of clarinets, bassoons, and horns in this symphony. Although the clarinet parts are notated in the key of the piece, the composer neither labeled them "in C" nor necessarily expected C clarinets to be used. Analysis of contemporary French scores shows that, in Paris, music notated in two flats was probably played on the B-flat clarinet.[55] Although the bassoon part never divides into more than two lines, and although only one partbook is extant in manuscript (see The Sources below), the surviving pairs of partbooks for bassoons in Méhul's symphonies Nos. 2, 3, and 4 show that four bassoons were used in these cases.[56] Thus, four bassoons were probably envisaged for the G Minor Symphony as well. The horn parts similarly never divide into more than two lines, but the survival of twin partbooks for horns in Méhul's symphonies Nos. 1, 3, and 4 may possibly be evidence for performance here also by four horns rather than two, but there is no definite indication of this.

Tempo

An analysis of the metronome indications of various composers cited in the leaflet *Notice sur le métronome de J. Maelzel* (Paris, Imprimerie Constant-Chantpie, ca. 1816) shows that "French speeds for given Italian terms were the quickest" of any in Europe.[57] This preference for brilliance was reported in the German press, which opined that all was played "more or less too quickly" at the Conservatoire.[58] Maelzel's table gives two sample tempos allegedly provided by Méhul: *Allegro moderato* in common time: half-note is between 72 and 88; *Allegro* in common time: half-note is 96. In the G Minor Symphony, therefore, the Allegro should perhaps be played with half-note about 90; the Andante should maintain a steady forward impetus and not dwell over details; the Menuet (for which the original printed full score lacks "Moderato") should be in scherzo tempo; and the Final perhaps with half-note played at 100.

Notation

The present editor believes that Méhul's diminuendo signs, like Beethoven's, relate spatially to the proportions of a given measure to indicate the desired duration of the expression. This edition, therefore, maintains the relative length of both crescendo and diminuendo signs. For the latter, there should be "an intensification of tone declining at a perceptible rate"[59] rather than simply a short stress or a long diminuendo.

Méhul's slender wedges in the autograph—more like dashes—obviously signify conventional staccato. Although the autograph contains no dots, the original edition of score and parts, perhaps with Méhul's approval, sometimes uses dots as an apparent alternative to dashes.

The Sources

Four sources were used in the preparation of this edition of Méhul's G Minor Symphony: the autograph of the first movement, measures 1–273, Bibliothèque Nationale MS 2323 (pp. 1–20) is Source A; the manuscript parts, Bibliothèque Nationale MS 17517, are Source MP; the first printed full score is designated as Source S; and the first printed "Paris" parts as Source P. A fifth source, the set of parts issued by Breitkopf & Härtel, was presumably prepared outside Méhul's control and, therefore, was not utilized in the present edition.[60]

Bibliothèque Nationale MS 2323 (pp. 1–20) (Source A) consists of five unbound folded leaves. Each page carries twenty staves and measures approximately 26 centimeters by 34.5 centimeters. The autograph is entitled "Simphonie No. I" (see Plate II) and contains measures 1–273 of the first movement. This manuscript source served as printer's copy for the first printed full score; the printer's pagination marks are still visible on the manuscript, and Méhul's order of staves was used by the original publisher (see Plate III). In publication, small changes were made in the horn parts in measures 95–100 and 135–41 (as discussed below in the Critical Notes). The first page of the autograph has a single full-sized leaf (the verso of which is blank) placed over it and attached at each corner. The original first page underneath presented an earlier version of measures 9–12; this is edited as Appendix 1 of the present volume. Parallel amendments were made by the composer in measures 118–22 (pages 9 and 10 of the manuscript), again by means of an overlaid staved sheet.[61]

Bibliothèque Nationale MS 17517 (Source MP) comprises twenty-two partbooks in the hand of various copyists with a few emendations in the composer's hand. The dimensions of the paper are similar to those of the autograph score, but each page holds only sixteen staves. Each manuscript partbook is identified by instrument, as below; all are entitled "Simphonie No. I [or "No. I Simphonie"] par Mr Méhul," except for (vi) and (vii), entitled "Sinfonie de Méhul." For purposes of discussion here and in the Critical Notes, a number has been assigned to each partbook as follows:

"Violino principale" (i); "Violino 1°" (ii); "Violino 2do No. I" (pencil annotation: "j. h. habeneck Sauvageot")[62] (iii); "Violino 2do No. [blank]" (smaller paper size; lacks measures 258–61 of the first movement) (iv); "Violino 2do" (v); "alto" (vi); "alto" (music begins on page 1) (vii); "alto" (page 1 is title page) (viii); "Basso No. I" (in crayon: "Norblin Chapuis")[63] (ix); "Nr 2 Basso" (x); "N. 3 Basso" (xi); "Violoncello et contrabasso" (xii); "Flutte 1re" (xiii); "Flutte 2de" (xiv); "Hautbois 1°" (xv); "Hautbois 2do" (xvi); "Clarinetto I^{o}" (xvii); "Clarinetto 2do" (xviii); "Fagotti" (xix); "Corno I^{o}" (xx); "Corno 2do" (xxi); "Timballes" (has duplicate page stuck over original one) (xxii).

Parts MPiv, MPvi, and MPxii were probably made after 1815. The supporting evidence is that cuts in the last movement between measures 72 and 93 and measures 235 and 247 were incorporated directly and silently. They correspond exactly to conventional cuts in all the other parts. Partbooks MPviii and MPix still have their *collettes* in place; the first is part of a government pro-forma, bearing the Bourbon crown and fleur-de-lys, while the second pro-forma refers to "S[on]. A[ltesse]. R[oyale]. MONSIEUR." Therefore, the cuts (seen in the other early partbooks by the wax marks that had stuck the *collettes*) can be dated to after 1815, and so partbooks MPiv, MPvi, and MPxii were not used in this edition. On the other hand, it is almost certain from details of phrasing that MPvii, MPviii, MPxv, and MPxvi were made from Source A. Indeed the horn parts, MPxx and MPxxi, were first copied to follow the original reading of Source A at measures 95ff. and 135ff. of the first movement and later altered with *collettes* (two of which are in Méhul's hand) to the published version. They can thus be dated 1809 (the year of publication) or before. The MP wind parts sometimes clarify readings such as in the Menuet, measures 80–84 (see Critical Notes below), and their dynamic markings in the Trio are sometimes unique. These presumably relate to the now-lost autograph of that movement.

The title page of the original edition of the printed full score (Source S) reads as follows: "SIMPHONIE / en Partition / Composée par / MÉHUL / No. [blank] / . . . / A PARIS / Chez M. M. Chérubini, Méhul, Kreutzer, Rode & Boieldieu / Rue de Richelieu, No. 76, vis-à-vis celle Ménars."[64] Plate numbers 641, 645, and 646 appear here, but inside pages bear only 641 (see Plate III). The first edition in full score of Méhul's Second Symphony, D major, has plate number 645. The above title page was thus intended to serve three symphonies, only two of which were ever issued.

The announcements of issue were carried in the *Journal de l'empire*, 14 January 1810, page 4, and in the *Journal général de la littérature de France*, xiii (Paris, Strasbourg, 1810), premier cahier (i.e., January 1810), page 30. They are for score and parts of both symphonies, No. 1 in G minor and No. 2 in D major. However, it is likely that the publication actually took place towards the end of 1809. This hypothesis is based on two facts. First, it is a matter of record that in 1810 Méhul defaulted in his contractual obligation to publish a major work with the publishing house in which he had a share, the firm of Chérubini, Méhul et al.[65] Second, the score of Kreutzer's opera *Aristippe*, which appeared in September 1809, bears this firm's imprint, with the closely proximate plate number 648.[66]

The publishing house of Chérubini, Méhul, Kreutzer, Rode and Boieldieu had been founded in 1802, and it operated for nine years. Since the firm existed to serve the interests of the participant composers, we may assume a high degree of communication between them and the engravers. A comparison of the score with the autograph of the first movement shows that the standard of accuracy is quite good. However, there are many errors of detail. For example, Méhul seems to have made small changes in the proofing, of which the most important are in measures 6, 7, and 11 (see Critical Notes).

For the present edition the copy of the original issue of the Symphony at the British Library was used. Libraries in addition to those cited by RISM which hold this first edition are the Conservatoire Royal de Musique in Liège and the Haags Gemeentemuseum in The Hague. The copy at the Bibliothèque Nationale (AC.e.^{10}.914(1)) can be identified as a later issue of the first edition by its new title page (which is reproduced in Brancour, *Méhul*, page 89), by the absence of plate numbers, and by the change of publisher. The title page of the later issue is headed by an elaborate device designed by Isabey, containing a shield, wreath, arrows, lyre, and pedestal, and reads as follows: "Simphonies / A Grand Orchestre / Dédiées / A S. Ex.^{ce} Monseigneur le Comte / REGNAUD DE SAINT-JEAN-D'ANGÉLY, / Ministre d'État, / . . . / Par / MÉHUL, / Membre de la Légion d'Honneur, de l'Institut et du Conservatoire./ N^o. [blank] à Paris Prix 10 Fr. / Au Magasin de Musique Rue de Richelieu No. 76."[67] Page 1 is blank; the music appears on pages 2–67. The issue probably post-dates the 1811 demise of the publishing business of Chérubini, Méhul et al., when the assets were bought up by Frey.

The only libraries holding a set of the printed "Paris" parts (Source P) of this symphony are Palermo and Stockholm (as cited in RISM), the Conservatoire Royal de Musique in Liège, and the Haags Gemeentemuseum in The Hague. In the preparation of the present edition, photocopies of the set from The Hague were used, except for a missing second clarinet part which was checked from a photocopy made from the Stockholm set.

The title page of Source P reads as follows: "SIMPHONIE / A Grand Orchestre / Par / MÉHUL / No. [blank] / . . . / A PARIS / Chez M. M. Chérubini, Méhul, Kreutzer, Rode & Boieldieu / Rue de Richelieu, No. 76 vis-à-vis celle Ménars."[68] Plate numbers 640, 643, and 647 appear here, but the parts themselves show only 640. Since the parts of Symphony No. 2 in D bear 643, presumably 647 was assigned to the parts of the Third Symphony which, like their companion full score, never appeared. The parts were issued at the same time as the printed score (S), and the standard of engraving is equally good. Méhul seems to have added or amended details in proofing (for example, the first movement in mm. 6, 7, and 11, and perhaps in mm. 127–130, as cited in the Critical Notes).

Editorial Principles

First movement, mm. 1 to 273

The editor has used the autograph (A) as principal text but compared it with the manuscript parts (MP) and the printed score (S) and parts (P). Selected variant readings in the secondary sources are listed. Source A itself contains some inconsistencies of phrasing and expression but only two instances of illogicity in pitch or rhythm. These are in measures 6 and 7 (clarinet) and 11 (viola, flute), where the printed sources are likelier. Editorial ties and slurs appear as dashed curves, and other editorial additions are shown in square brackets. Those deriving from sources MP, S, or P are explained in the Critical Notes. The few emendations of Méhul's markings are also explained here. Méhul does not generally repeat an accidental in one part at a different octave within the measure, but he does repeat an accidental tied over a barline. In accord with modern convention, we have adopted the opposite principle in each case. Méhul's cautionary accidentals are omitted when deemed unnecessary by contemporary practice. The abbreviations "dol" and "cres" or the word "crescendo" have been replaced by "dolce" and "cresc.," and woodwind double stems have been replaced by single stems and "a 2" directives.

First movement, mm. 274 to 286, and last three movements

For measures 274 to 286 only an earlier version is available in autograph. See the partial reproduction in Plate I, and the edition in Appendix 2.

The editor regards the manuscript parts (MP), the printed parts (P), and the printed score (S) as potentially equal in authority, all presumably deriving from an autograph. There are many detail differences (the majority being slight) between S and P. In the present edition there is a bias towards S as the main text, owing to its consistency and fidelity to A in the first movement. Yet a reading in which MP and P together oppose S will often prevail; in general, a given reading in two sources will provide the resulting text (errors apart). In the Critical Notes, a reading in the mentioned source(s) implies that all unmentioned sources contain the reading which is adopted in the present score. No obvious misprints are listed; editorial ties and slurs appear as dashed curves, and all other editorial additions appear in square brackets.

Méhul's slender wedges in his autograph score (given as thick wedges in this edition) were well reproduced in S. For the engravers, at least, there was certainly some synonimity between wedges and dots; the last movement sometimes has the former in S and the latter in P. Yet dots appear in the Andante in S, and these have been exclusively adopted for this movement alone. The modern forms "dolce," "cresc.," and "pizz." replace various original forms. The same principles towards accidentals and editorial emendations have been followed here as are stated above. In the second and fourth movements, Méhul's frequent grouping of eighth-notes in threes has been respected, since it has clear motivic significance. Beam groupings have otherwise been tacitly regularized among similar passages.

Critical Notes

The following abbreviations are used for sources cited in the Critical Notes: A = autograph manuscript; MP = manuscript parts; S = first printed score; P = first printed parts. Full formal bibliographical identification and validation of these sources has been given above in the section The Sources.

The following instrumental designation abbreviations (in score order) are used in the Critical Notes: fl., ob., cl., bsn., hn., timp., vn., vla., d-bass, str.

And finally, M. = measure (bar); Mm. = measures.

Pitches are designated in the usual way: C is the lowest cello note, D its upper neighbor, c the lowest viola note, d its upper neighbor, c' is middle C, and c" the octave above c'. The term "accent" below refers to the stress/decrescendo sign discussed above under Performance Practice: Notation.

Allegro

Original instrument designations, from the top downwards: VV, al, fl, h, cl, Cors en Si, Fag, b, timb. en Sol. (See Plate II.)

Mm. 1–13, two versions of A exist, one stuck over the other. The first version of mm. 9–12 is edited in Appendix 1, and the final version is given in Plate III. Mm. 6–7, cl., A has whole-notes followed by quarter-rest. M. 8, hn. I, P omits second note. M. 10, vn. I, fourth note stac. in MPi, ii, P. M. 11, fl., A, MPxiii, xiv begin with half-rest; vla., A, MPvii, viii begin with half-rest (cf. mm. 118–22). Mm. 16–24, all parts, phrasing at first identical in A, MP, S, but after m. 16, sources vary, sometimes sweeping slur over to next m.; only adopted emendations of A are noted. M. 17, vla., A, MPvii, viii, P extend slur by one note. Mm. 20–24, ob., bsn., A, S, MPx (mm. 22, 23) extend slurs by one note. Mm. 25, 27, vn. I, stac. in P, S. Mm. 25, 27–31, vn. II, MPiii, v slur first three of each group of four notes. M. 26, vn. I, stac. in S. Mm. 32–35, vn. I and II, bass, have pencil accents by each group of four eighths in MPii, iii, ix, x, xi. Mm. 39–41, bsn., S doubles bass. Mm. 59–67, all parts, many detail differences of slurring in MP, P, S both here and in subsequent statements, not noted. M. 81, ob. I, stac. in MPxv, S. Mm. 83–84, vn. I, A does not extend slur to half-note, although longer slurs appear in all sources for simultaneous phrase in vla., cl., bsn. Mm. 91, 93, ob. II, cl. II, bsn. II, slurs in P. Mm. 91–95, vla., all sources except A indicate div. Mm. 95–98, hns., A, MPxx, xxi originally had rests. Pencil alterations to A and autograph *collettes* in MPxx, xxi give result as in S, used here. Mm. 98–99, bass, pencil dim. in MPx. Mm. 99–100, hns., MPxx, xxi, P, have whole-rests, while A amends inked rests with pencil to reading in S, adopted here. M. 101, bass, MPx, xi have initial f' instead of rest. Mm. 101–103, vla., MPvi has "légèrement" and stac. on downward run. M. 114, ob. II, S gives first note as a'. Mm. 115–116, vla., lower note of chord is a in S, P. Mm. 118–122, two versions exist, one stuck over the other. The rejected one is musically parallel to that in Appendix 1, relative to mm. 9–12. M. 122, vn. II, stac. in P, S. M. 126, cl. I, dynamic in S. Mm. 127–130, vn. I, stac. on each f' in P. Mm. 127–129, vn. II, as for mm. 27–31. Mm. 131–133, ob. II, slurs in P. Mm. 131–134, cl. II, bsn. II, slurs in MPxviii, xix, P. M. 134, fl. II, ob. I, vn. I and II, last two notes slurred in S; slur in A has been erased. Mm. 135–141, hns., A originally had rests, later amended in ink; MPxx, xxi have *collettes*. M. 146, vla., stac. in S. M. 148, bsn., A omits rests. M. 150, vn. I, stac. in S. M. 154, bass, stac. in P, S. M. 157, vn. I, bracketed accidental is given in P. M. 158, vn. II, stac. in S. Mm. 159–164, ob. II, slurs in P. Mm. 170–171, vn. I, bracketed accidentals given in S. M. 175, vla., bracketed accidental given in S. M. 178, cl. II, slur in P; bsn. II, dynamic in S, slur in P. Mm. 188–189, vn. I and II, accents in MPi, ii, iii, v, P, S; ob., cl., accents in S. M. 190, cl. I, vn., accents in S; ob. I, stac. in MPxv, P. Mm. 193, 195, vn. II, stac. in MPv, P. M. 194, vla., slur extension in MPvii, P. Mm. 199, 201, ob. II, cl. II, bsn. I, slurs in MP and/or P. Mm. 199–203, vla., MPvii, viii, P, notation indicates div. M. 217, obs., cls., S gives third diad as b'-flat/g'. M. 221, ob II, S, P give third note as f'-sharp (this could be a late alteration by Méhul). M. 225, bsn., MPxix has dynamic marking ff in pencil. M. 231, bsn., MPxix, P have dynamic marking f. Mm. 234–241, vn. II, these four slurs do not quite sweep over in A. Mm. 235, 237, 239, 241, vn. II, MPiii, v slur first three of each group of four notes. M. 242, fl. II, slur in P. Mm. 242–245, bass, MP, P, S have single stems. M. 243–245, ob. II, cl. II, slurs in MPxvi, xviii, P. M. 253, vn. I, MPi, ii insert d' in second and third chords. Mm. 255, 257, 259, 261, vn. II, as for mm. 235–241. M. 260 note 2–m. 262 note 1, bsn., the eight-note phrase has single stems in A, and S says "1er" but MPxix, P demand both players. M. 262, 263, fl. II, slurs in MPxiv, P. Mm. 263–265, ob. II, cl. II, slurs in MPxvi, xviii, P. Mm. 274–286, only an earlier version is extant in autograph; see Appendix 2. M. 279, vn. I, d' in last chord in S only.

Andante

Mm. 4–5, vn. II, slur in MPiii, v, but P as for fl. M. 7, fl., slur one note longer in S, and absent from MPxiii, P.; ob., slur one note longer in S. M. 8, ob., no stac. in P. Mm. 13–14, bsn., MPxix, P imply "a 2." M. 15, fl., slur eighth longer in MPxiii, P. Mm. 25–26, vn. II, hairpin in P. Mm. 27–28, bsn., slur one note longer in S. M. 31, vn. I, slur one note shorter in S. M. 32, vn. II, slur in P only. Mm. 40–44, fl., slur whole m. longer in S. M. 43, vn. II, slur begins note later in MPiii, S. Mm. 54–55, vn. I, S joins last two slurs into one. M. 65, vla., S reverses note-values. Mm. 72–76, S omits fl. II. Mm. 74–75, vn. I, as for mm. 54–55. M. 84, vla., slur one note shorter in P, S. M. 89 note 2–m. 90 note 1, bsn., bass, slurs one note longer in P. M. 104, vla., MPvii, viii have pencilled stac. on all three notes. Mm. 113–114, S omits first five notes. M. 119, vn. I, P has shorter accent. Mm. 119–122, vla., MPvii, viii have pencilled cresc. Mm. 132–133, bsn. I, P slurs each m. separately. M. 133 note 3–m. 135, vn. I, MPi has pencilled stac. M. 134, bass, S phrases in sixes. M. 137, vla., first e' is flatted in S. Mm. 155, 156, bsn., extension of slurs over barline is editorial. M. 163, vla., P omits decresc. Mm. 164–166, vla., MPvii indicates pencilled "fort," then decresc. Mm. 164–165, all sources use this cello notation. M. 176–177, vla., bsn., bass, stac. in P only (some dots, some wedges). Mm. 180–181, bsn., bass., stac. in P only. M. 182, ob. II, MPxvi, P slur g", a", b"-flat. Mm. 183–184, fl. I, MPxiii, P slur whole phrase. Mm. 200, 201, bsn., slurs a note shorter in MPxix, P. Mm. 210–211, vn. I, S omits d''' from slur. M. 213, vn. I, S slur as for vla. M. 217, cl. II, MPxviii, P attach both notes to next slur. Mm. 221–225, vla., div. in MPvii, viii, P indicated by two staves. M. 221, bass, MPix, x, xi omit tie. Mm. 239–240, fl., slur not in MPxiii; cl., slur not in MPxviii, P. Mm. 239–241, bass, notation ambiguous in S; MPx, xi lack d-bass separation.

Menuet

Only a player's mark in MPi and P give "moderato." M. 1, bass, "Soli" not in S. M. 42, ob., "dolce" in S. Mm. 45–46, no cresc. in most MP. Mm. 50, 51, vla., MPvii, viii, P slur each m. separately. M. 60, vn. I, MPi, ii have "mp" in pencil. M. 64, vn. I, S gives f"-sharp. Mm. 75–76, cl., S follows sequence set in mm. 71–72, stopping after the fourth note of each phrase. Mm. 80–84, most MP indicate an original dim. from ff to p, as do P ob. and cl. II parts, however this dynamic scheme is erased in crayon in most MP str. parts in favor of f or ff, the dynamics found in S and (except ob. and cl. II) P. Mm. 81–83, vla., P has dynamic marking f against each third note. Mm. 81–84, cl. I, II, S omits all four chords. Mm. 89–90, as for mm. 45–46, no cresc. in most MP though i adds cresc. in pencil. M. 148, vn. I, bass, no dynamic in most MP and S. M. 155, ob. II, first note g' in S. Mm. 163–164, hns., accents in S. M. 171, vla., change from div. to double stops notated with two staves in MPvii, viii, P.

Final

"Agitato" not in MP; P have spelling "finale."
M. 13, hn., stac. in P only. All unbracketed stac. marks have at least one source, but these are not noted below. Mm. 29–35, vla., first two of each set of four eighths are slurred in MPvii, P. Mm. 33–34, no cello-bass separation in MPix, x, P. M. 34, bass, MPxi omits c', d', e'-flat entirely. Mm. 39, 45, vn. I, dynamic marking f in MPi, P. M. 51, vn. II, S omits upper note of chord. Mm. 60, 62, bass, P gives "pizz." Mm. 68, 70, bass, tutti play in MPix, x, xi, P. M. 77, vn. I, S has g"-natural as note four. M. 83, bsn., MPxix trill on first note. M. 84, fls., trill in MPxiii, xiv. Mm. 89, 91, vla., S has g-natural as note three. M. 94, bsn. I, and M. 95, vn. II, S extends slur over barline (cf. m. 254). Mm. 113–114, cl. I, ob. I, tie in P. M. 120, bsn., S has "p." Mm. 135, 137, cl. I, slurs in S. M. 139, vn. II, first two notes slurred in MPiii, v, P; bass, P has "ff" by new entry. Mm. 173–177, S has cello and d-bass playing double-stopped octaves. M. 177, timp., dim. begins one m. later in S. M. 202, vla., e'-flat not in S. M. 214, bsn., last three notes are g in P. M. 242, fl., MPxiii has b"-flat. Mm. 254, 256, vn. II, S extends slur by one note. M. 261, ob. I, "dolce" in MPxv only. Mm. 264–265, vla., S omits slurs. Mm. 269–270, vn. I and II, no cresc. in MPi, ii, iii, v, P, and cresc. half-note later in S. M. 295, vn. II, first two notes slurred in MPv, P. M. 296, hn., dynamic in P only with chord two. Mm. 300–303, vla., single stems in all sources. Mm. 306–307, bass, MPx, xi, S slur first two notes.

Acknowledgments

I am very grateful to the librarians of the Haags Gemeentemuseum, The Hague, and the Kungliga Musikalisca Akademiens Bibliotek, Stockholm, for provision of photocopies; to M. François Lesure and M. Jean-Michel Nectoux of the Bibliothèque Nationale, Paris; to the Department of Printed Books, Bodleian Library, Oxford; to the British Library; and to Herr Andreas Göpfert of the Gewandhaus zu Leipzig. Advice and assistance was generously given by Yvette Billingham, Clive Brown, Warwick Edwards, John Gage, Edward Higginbottom, Michel Noiray, Robert Pascall, Keith Pollard, Julian Rushton, Els Visscher, and Julian Webb. M. Elizabeth C. Bartlet furnished particular help from her knowledge of the Méhul source materials and has my special thanks. Anthony Caston undertook the task of copying the edited score, and I owe his enthusiasm and critical eye a warm debt of gratitude. For research funding and the provision of sabbatical leave, I thank the School of Fine Arts and Music, University of East Anglia.

David Charlton

Notes

1. Anonymous letter to the editor in *Revue musicale* (publiée par M. Fétis), deuxième série, 4, tome 7, livraison 8 [27 March] 1830: 237.

2. Full details of Méhul's musical output are included in the present writer's article "Méhul, Etienne-Nicolas" in *The New Grove Dictionary of Music and Musicians*. Many detailed amendments will be found in the unpublished thesis by M. Elizabeth C. Bartlet, "Etienne Nicolas Méhul and Opera During the French Revolution, Consulate and Empire: A Source, Archival and Stylistic Study" (Ph.D. diss., University of Chicago, 1982).

3. In 1817 Weber wrote: "The least well known [in Germany] are *Adrien* and *Ariodant*, and the most popular *Une folie*, . . . *Héléna*, and *Les deux aveugles*, and most recently *Joseph*" (*Carl Maria von Weber Writings on Music*, trans. Martin Cooper, ed. John Warrack (Cambridge University Press, 1981), 209).

4. Bibliothèque Nationale MS 2271 (1).

5. Quoted from a sale catalogue in Arthur Pougin, *Méhul, sa vie, son génie, son caractère* (Paris, 1893), 303.

6. Barry S. Brook, *La symphonie française dans la seconde moitié du XVIIIe siècle*, 3 vols. (Paris, 1962), 1: 350, 468; 2: 265–339. See also Robert J. Macdonald, "François-Joseph Gossec" (Ph.D. diss., University of Michigan, 1968).

7. These statistics include repeat performances of the same work. All statistics here are taken from Constant Pierre, *Histoire du Concert Spirituel 1725–1790* (Paris, 1975), 313–44.

8. Brook, *La symphonie française*, 2: 90–91.

9. Pierre, *Histoire*, 66–68 and 343–44; *Les spectacles de Paris, et de toute la France* [for the year] 1792, "Concert Spirituel."

10. *Journal des théâtres*, second trimestre, no. 11, 6 Nivôse An III: 145. The attendance receipts for concerts could attain 10,000 *livres*. Details of first performances in Brook, *La symphonie française*, 1; 387f.

11. Boris Schwarz, "French Instrumental Music between the Revolutions, 1789–1830" (Ph.D. diss., Columbia University, 1950), 30–32. A revised edition of this study is in the press.

12. J. G. Prod'homme and E. de Crauzat, *Les Menus Plaisirs du Roi, l'Ecole Royale et le Conservatoire de Musique* (Paris, 1929), 41–46 and 124–25. The auditorium of Jean Monnet's theater built in 1752 for the Foire Saint-Laurent was both visually and acoustically worth preserving and was transferred to the Menus Plaisirs du Roi at some time after 1762. It survived the fire of 1788 and was eventually reinstalled adjacent to the rue Bergère between 1784 and 1802. When this part of the Menus Plaisirs became the new Conservatoire of Music in 1795, the auditorium became the "Salle des Exercices."

13. *Mercure de France*, 17 March 1810, 179–82.

14. Schwarz, "French Instrumental Music," 39–40.

15. Rita Benton, "Pleyel's *Bibliothèque musicale*," *The Music Review* 36 (1975): 1–4.

16. Jérôme-Joseph de Momigny, *Cours complet d'harmonie et de composition*, 2 vols. (Paris, 1803–1806), 1: 307–82; 2: 387ff.

17. Usually assumed to be K. V. 550, but K. V. 183 had been published in 1798. The Conservatoire concert programs appear in Constant Pierre, *Le Conservatoire National de Musique et de Déclamation* (Paris, 1900).

18. From an undated manuscript in private possession. A German report on Méhul (*Allgemeine musikalische Zeitung*, 4, 17 March 1802) attributed to him an opinion of Mozart as "one of the greatest musical geniuses."

19. Anton Schindler, *Beethoven in Paris* (Münster, 1842), 3. See Schwarz, "French Instrumental Music," 136, and Alexander L. Ringer, "A French Symphonist at the Time of Beethoven: Etienne Nicolas Méhul," *Musical Quarterly* 37 (1951): 543–65.

20. *Le courrier des spectacles ou Journal des Théâtres*, 10 Pluviôse An V (29 January 1797): 3. For a discussion of the second review published in *Le courrier*, 20 Pluviôse An V (8 February 1797): 3, see Ringer, "A French Symphonist," 546–47. However, Ringer was unaware of Bibliothèque Nationale MS 2271 (4, 5).

21. Pierre, *Le Conservatoire National*, 477.

22. Edouard Gregoir, *Souvenirs artistiques*, 2 vols. (Brussels, Paris, 1888, 1889), 1: 156. The ballroom was the Salon des Redoutes. See *Journal de l'empire*, 2, 12, 23 January 1806; *Moniteur universel*, 1, 6, 30 January 1806.

23. *Journal de l'empire*, 7 November 1808, 3. Like all the French reviews of the time, this was published anonymously. Transcription in Pougin, *Méhul*, 299–300. Pougin gives "rue Mandar" for "cour Mandar" and is followed in this by later writers. "Lefèvre" was probably Théodore Lefèvre, a well-known orchestral violinist-leader and a founder of the Grenelle concerts.

24. *Journal de l'empire*, 23 November 1808, 4.

25. British Library, Department of Manuscripts, Egerton 23, fols. 166–67.

26. *Allgemeine musikalische Zeitung* 11 (23 August 1809): col. 751.

27. *Journal de l'empire*, 14 March 1809, 3.

28. *Journal de Paris*, 14 March 1809, 539–40.

29. *Journal de l'empire*, 29 March 1809, 3; *Journal de Paris*, 29 March 1809, 654–55; *Moniteur universel*, 30 March 1809, 355–56 (also in Pougin, *Méhul*, 302–303); *Courrier de l'Europe et des spectacles*, 4 April 1809, 3.

30. *Journal de l'empire*, 27 May 1809, 4.

31. Quoted from a sale catalogue in Pougin, *Méhul*, 303.

32. Watermark dating by M. Elizabeth C. Bartlet, privately communicated.

33. Archives Nationales, Paris, AJ 37.82 (7a).

34. Arthur Pougin, "Notice sur Méhul par Chérubini," *Rivista musicale italiana* 16 (1909): 759, 771.

35. *Revue musicale* (publiée par M. Fétis), deuxième série, 4, tome 7, livraison 5 (6 March 1830): 152–53.

36. A. Dandelot, *La Société des Concerts du Conservatoire (1828–1923)* (Paris, 1923), 148.

37. Alfred Dörffel, *Geschichte der Gewandhausconcerte zu Leipzig*, 2 vols. (Leipzig, 1881, 1884), 1: 38; *Allgemeine musikalische Zeitung* 12 (6 June 1810): col. 565.

38. *Allgemeine musikalische Zeitung* 12 (3 October 1810), "Intelligenz-Blatt," col. 41.

39. *Allgemeine musikalische Zeitung* 12 (19 December 1810): col. 1040. John Warrack's opinion, informally communicated, is that the writer was probably Friedrich Rochlitz.

40. *Allgemeine musikalische Zeitung* 40 (7 March 1838): cols. 167–68; 40 (2 May 1838): cols. 288–90.

41. From "Rückblick auf das Leipziger Musikleben im Winter 1837–1838," reprinted in *Gesammelte Schriften über Musik und Musiker von Robert Schumann*, ed. Martin Kreisig, 2 vols. (1914; reprint Farnborough, 1969), 1: 376. Two subsequent Gewandhaus performances took place on 5 March 1846, under Mendelssohn, and 12 March 1863, under Carl Reinecke.

42. *The Letters of Beethoven*, ed. and trans. Emily Anderson, 3 vols. (London 1961), 3: 1003, 1111.

43. *The Musical Examiner* 1 (1843): 85.

44. *Life and Letters of Sir Charles Hallé. Being An Autobiography, 1819–1860* (London, 1896), 357–61, entries from 29 December 1855 to 12 January 1856. He is the only writer to criticize the composer's workmanship, though he found that "the ideas are fresh and noble."

45. *The Musical World* 40 (15 March 1862): 170–71.

46. *The Times*, 3 May 1864, 7; reprinted in *The Musical World* 42 (7 May 1864): 301.

47. Hérold's two symphonies have recently been reprinted, with introductory essays: Barry S. Brook, ed., The Symphony 1720–1840, Series D, Volume 9: *Ferdinand Hérold 1791–1833 Two Symphonies.*, ed. Boris Schwarz (New York, London, 1981).

48. René Brancour, *Méhul* (Paris, [1912]), 109; Ringer, "A French Symphonist," 562–63. Compare also the tarantella rhythms of Mendelssohn's Fourth Symphony finale with those of the last movement of Méhul's Second Symphony.

49. Bibliothèque de l'Opéra, Paris, Registres de l'Opéra-

Comique. Comparative statistics of the sizes of Parisian orchestras are quoted and discussed in David Charlton, "Orchestration and Orchestral Practice in Paris 1789–1810" (Ph.D. diss., Cambridge University, 1973), chap. 2.

50. H. C. Robbins Landon, *Haydn at Eszterháza (1766–1790)* (London, 1978), 608.

51. Nicolas Lebègue, *Troisième livre d'orgue* (Paris, [1678–1685]); André Raison, *Second livre d'orgue* (Paris, 1714); Claude-Bénigne Balbastre, *Recueil de noëls* (Paris, 1770); Jean-Jacques Beauvarlet-Charpentier, *Douze noëls variés*, op. 13 (Paris, 1782). The melody and words are found in Henry Poulaille, *La grande et belle bible des noëls anciens*, 2 vols. (Paris, 1949), 2: 603.

52. Antoine Elwart, *Histoire de la Société des Concerts du Conservatoire* (Paris, 1860), 54.

53. Pierre, *Le Conservatoire National*, 460–70; Constant Pierre, *B. Sarrette et les origines du Conservatoire National de Musique et de Déclamation* (Paris, 1895), 192.

54. "Personnel des élèves / Déclamation dramatique de 1807 à 1812," Archives Nationales, Paris, AJ 37.87*, 235–37 and 261–67.

55. David Charlton, "Orchestration and Orchestral Practice," chap. 6. Even the manuscript clarinet partbooks of the present symphony are at concert pitch rather than transposed, but one finds the same rule applying elsewhere in Paris at the time, for example, the manuscript parts of works given at the Opéra. The players were accustomed to transpose at sight.

56. Bibliothèque Nationale, Département de la Musique, MS 17518, D 17595, D 17596.

57. The metronome table is reproduced from Bibliothèque Nationale 8°.B.2898(4) in Charlton, "Orchestration and Orchestral Practice," 69, from where the citation is also drawn.

58. *Allgemeine musikalische Zeitung* 11 (June 1809): col. 604; see also 11 (August 1809): col. 748.

59. Hugh Macdonald, "Two Peculiarities of Berlioz's Notation," *Music & Letters* 50 (1969): 32–36. The author deals with the same phenomenon in Berlioz, who, however, was clearly not an innovator in his use of the sign, as is suggested by Macdonald. The importance of proportional notation is understood by the editors of the Beethoven *Werke: Neue Ausgabe*, who have introduced the term "Raumverteilung" ("spatial distribution") and try to reproduce it in their editions.

60. Announcement as in note 38. Martin Kreisig gives the actual publication date as July 1810 in *Gesammelte Schriften über Musik und Musiker von Robert Schumann*, 2: 420. Title page reads: "Mehul, F. [sic], Sinfonie a gr. Orchestre. No. 1. 3 Thlr.," plate number 1602.

61. The verso of the *collette* on p. 10 reveals the words "chant fune[bre]." This is the title of an unpublished work by Méhul, Bibliothèque Nationale, Département de la Musique, MS 2295.

62. The document named in note 54, p. 263, shows that Joseph Habeneck, the younger brother of François, sat at the first desk of second violins in 1813–1814, while Sauvageot sat at the second desk at that time.

63. The document named in note 54, p. 264, shows that Norblin and Chapuis were still first desk players in 1813–1814. Norblin played concertos at the Conservatoire in 1804, 1806, and 1811. See Pierre, *Le Conservatoire Nationale*, 481, 485, 491.

64. From the copy in the British Library. "1" is entered in ink in the blank space.

65. Ringer, "A French Symphonist," 553. The standard history of this publishing house is in Constant Pierre, *Le magasin de musique à l'usage des fêtes nationales et du Conservatoire* (Paris, 1895), chap. 6.

66. Announcement of issue in *Journal de l'empire*, 1 October 1809. Month of appearance kindly communicated by François Lesure.

67. Michel-Louis-Etienne Regnaud [or Regnault], 1761 or 1762–1819. The earlier birth date given in *Encyclopedia Britannica*, the later in *Napoléon au Conseil d'Etat*, ed. Jean Bourdon (Paris, 1963), 324. Regnaud was an assistant of Napoleon at the *coup* of 18 Brumaire and was president of the Council of State from 1802 until the fall of the Empire.

68. From the copy in the Haags Gemeentemuseum, The Hague. "1" is entered in ink in the blank space.

Plate I. Autograph manuscript of the previously unknown version of the first movement, mm. 282–86. B.N. MS 2323, p. 22, 26 cm. x 34.5 cm. (Courtesy Bibliothèque Nationale, Paris). See Appendix 2, pp. 104–106.

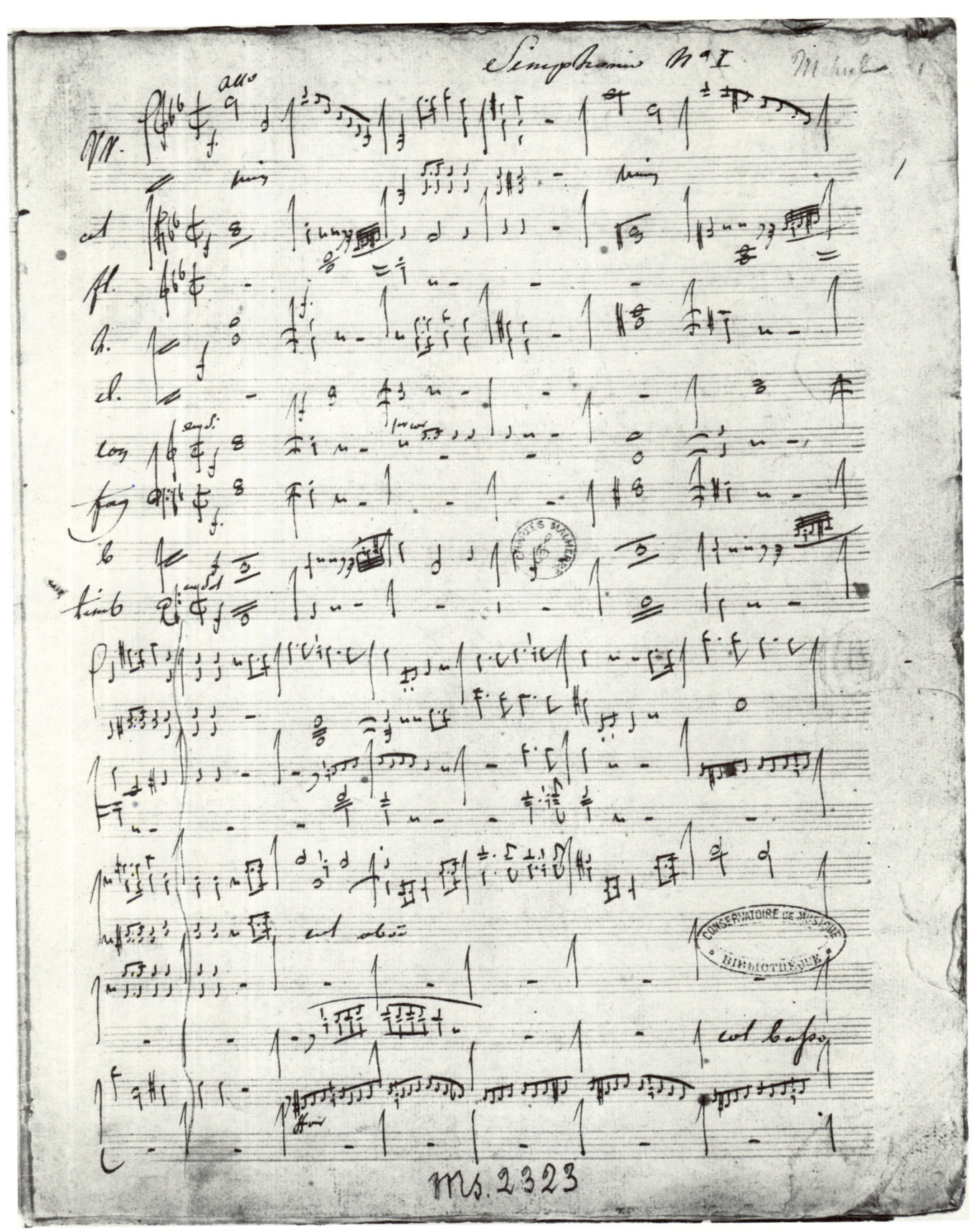

Plate II. Autograph manuscript of the "Simphonie No. 1," intermediate version of the first movement, mm. 1–13. B.N. MS 2323, p. 1, 26 cm. x 34.5 cm. (Courtesy Bibliothèque Nationale, Paris)

Plate III. First edition of the score, published by the firm of Chérubini, Méhul, Kreutzer, Rode & Boieldieu. (Courtesy British Library, London)

Symphony No. 1 in G Minor

* Clarinets in B♭ were probably used. See Preface, p. xiii.

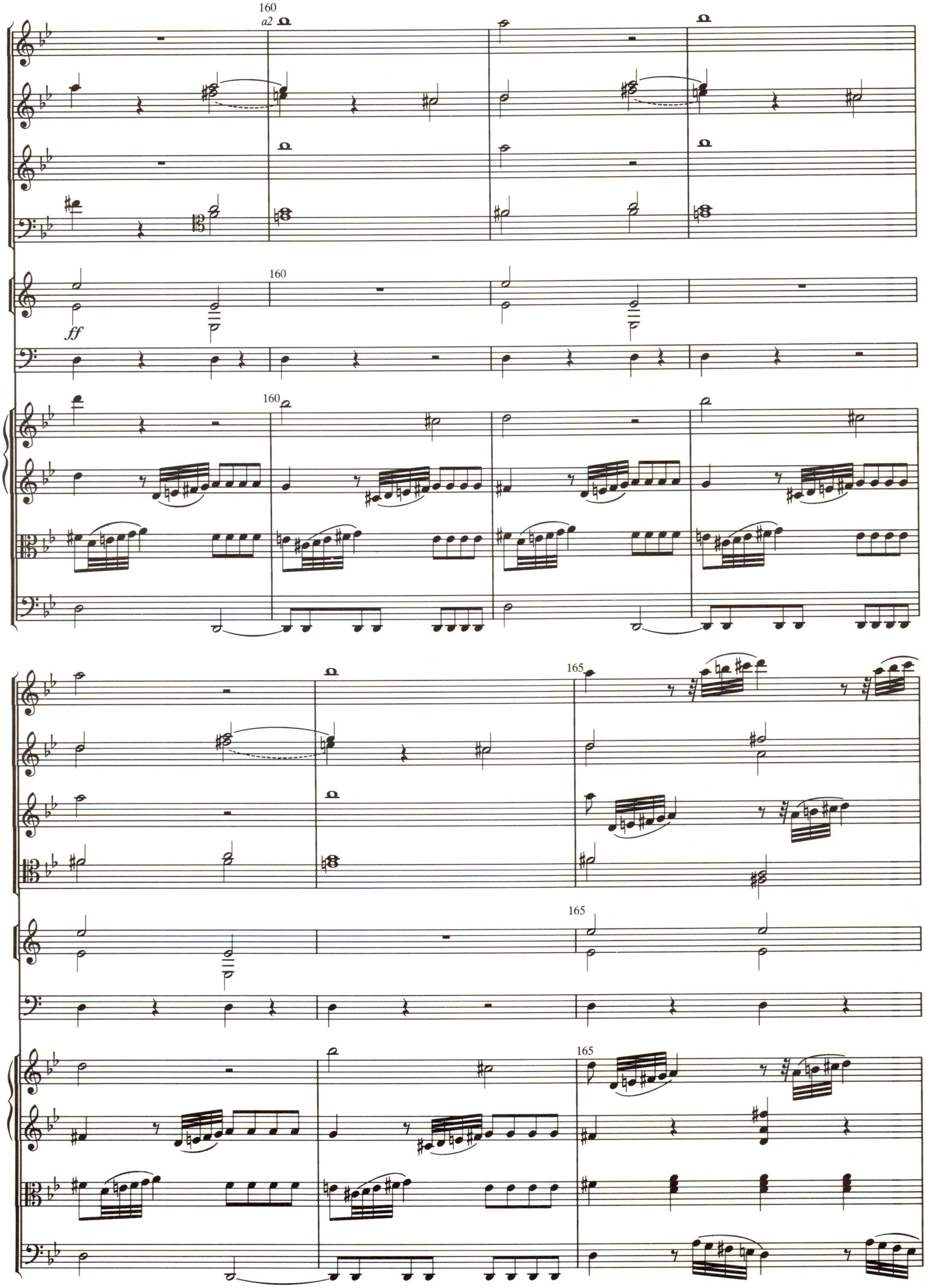
160
a2
160
ff
160
165
165
165

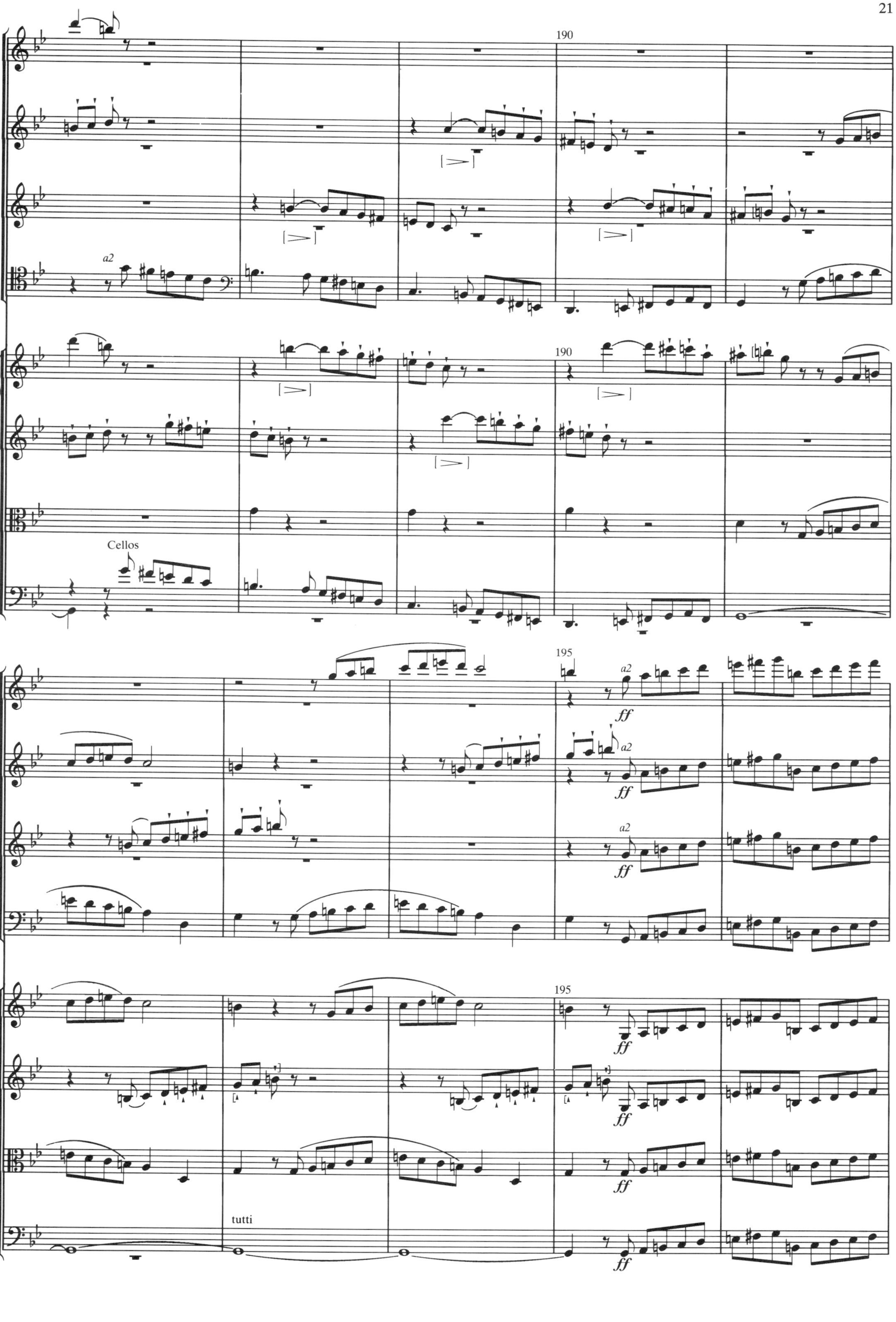
190
a2
Cellos
190
195
a2
ff
195
tutti

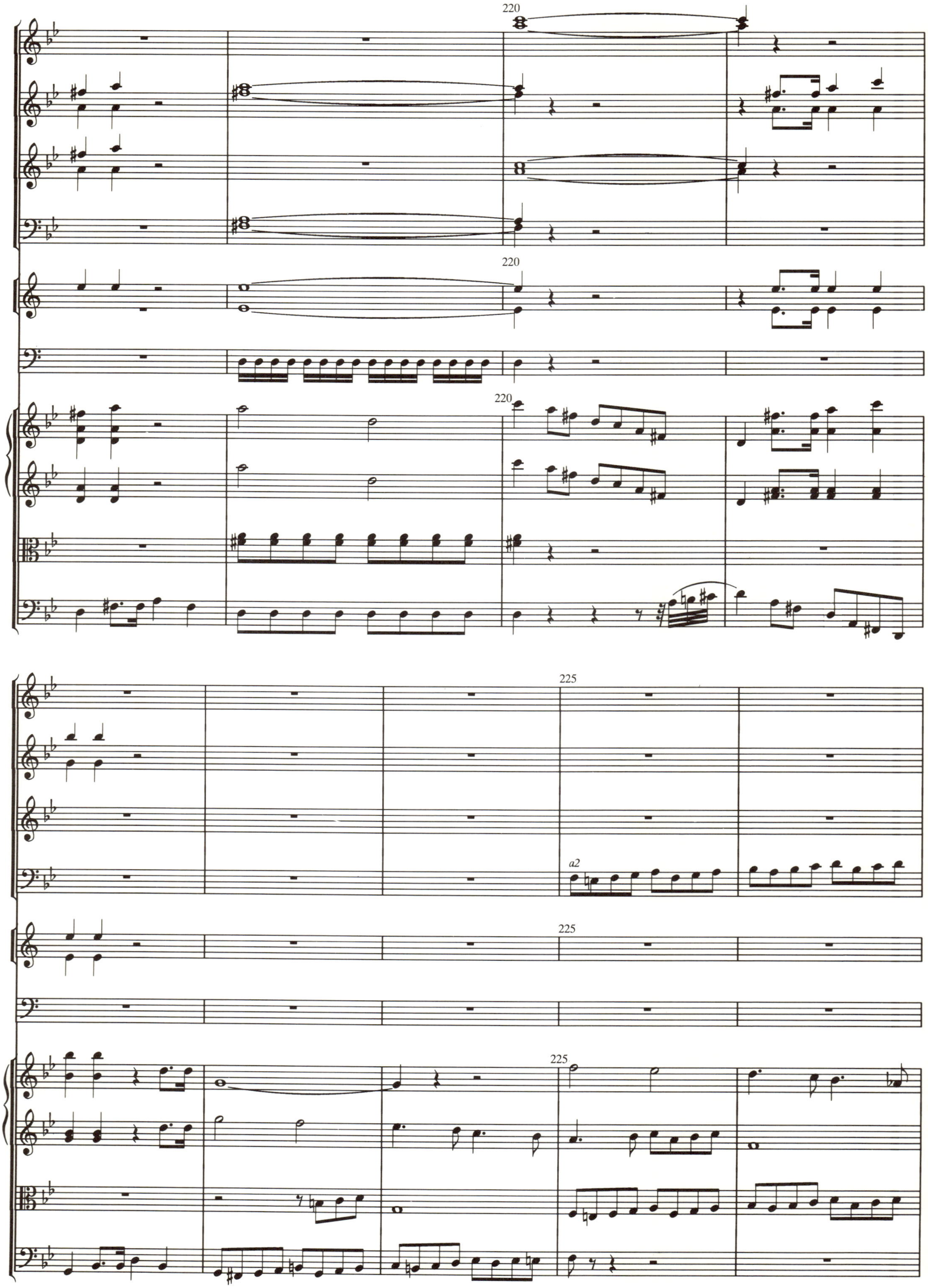
220
220
220
a2
225
225
225

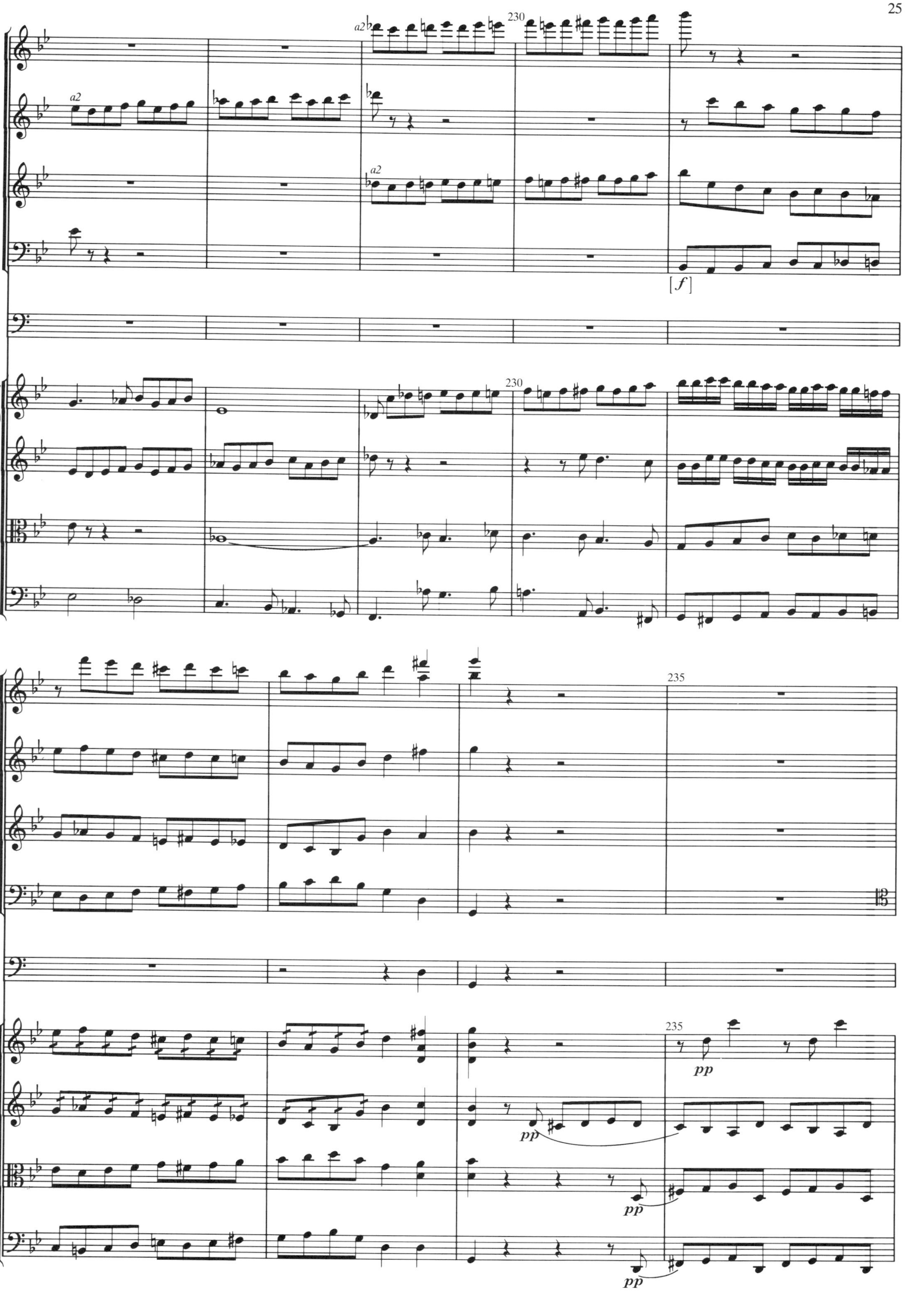

a2
a2
230
a2
[f]
230
235
235
pp
pp
pp

35

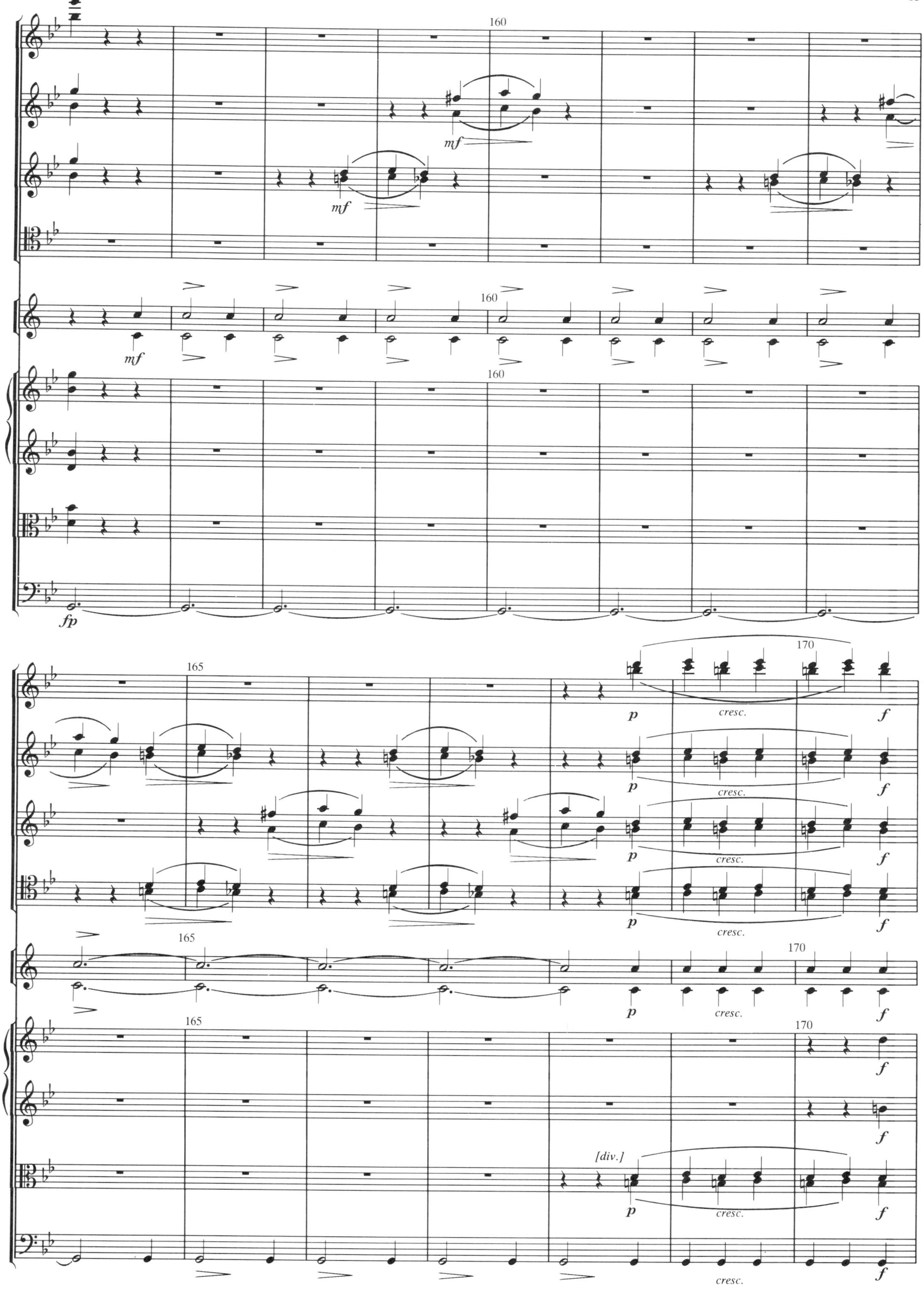
160
mf
fp
165
170
p
cresc.
f
[div.]

FINAL
Allegro agitato

98

Appendix 2

Appendix 1

Appendix 1

As explained in The Sources section of the Preface, the autograph score of Méhul's Symphony in G Minor (Bibliothèque Nationale MS 2323) contains the first movement only. But this manuscript comprises elements that were written down at several different times. Whereas pages 1–20 of the manuscript, used as printer's copy, present in general the composer's final thoughts, evidence of continuing refinement of the composition occurs on pages 1, 9, and 10. Here Méhul fastened newer music paper over rejected portions of his score. Appendix 1 is an edition of the superseded part of the rejected first page of MS 2323; the newly substituted page fastened over it is shown in Plate II; and that the composer was still not quite satisfied with mm. 6, 7, and 11 of *this* version may be seen by comparing Plate II with Plate III (the first printed score) and the present edition, p. 2.

The degree of musical improvement between the rejected first page, seen in Appendix 1, and the final version needs hardly be stressed. Méhul's injection of a dotted rhythm (mm. 9, 11) seems to connect inevitably between those already present in m. 8 and m. 12. His redesign of the violin parts in m. 10 and m. 12 enables there to be a finely logical building of tension from the descending line of a third, g" to e-flat" (mm. 9–10), through a descending fifth, c'" to f"-sharp (mm. 11–12), to the plunging arpeggio of mm. 13–15.

The composer's pencil sketching of part of these improvements is indicated in Appendix 1 by means of bracketed notes. His changes to mm. 118–122 of the first movement, effected by attaching new score paper to pp. 9 and 10, bring that passage into conformity with mm. 9–12. Formerly the music was as for Appendix 1, transposed into B-flat minor.

Appendix 2

If pages 1–20 of MS 2323 present us with the final episodes in the evolution of the first movement, or at least mm. 1–273 inclusive, pages 21–22 of the same manuscript take us back to an altogether earlier compositional stage. This single autograph leaf contains mm. 273–286 inclusive. Plate I shows the concluding measures of the movement in this version, while Appendix 2 is an edition of both pages 21 and 22.

Although the overall dimensions of the leaf in question are the same as the rest of MS 2323, the staff rule is narrower. The watermark, a cross under an inverted hemisphere, appears to be incomplete and has not yet been identified for dating purposes. It is, however, clear that the leaf is the only surviving evidence for an early version of the Symphony in G Minor scored for a larger orchestra than that revealed by any other source. Abbreviated instrument labels show that Méhul is writing here for four horns, two trumpets and a trombone, whereas the brass parts in the published form of the Symphony can be played on two horns only.

Two main indications suggest that the leaf antedates the rest of MS 2323. The first is a sign added at the foot of page 21 requesting that mm. 276 and 277 be repeated, as they are in fact in the coda of the Symphony as published. The second indication is the use of the abbreviation "b" for bassoons, not "fag" as in the rest of MS 2323. A systematic review of Méhul's earlier autographs—*Uthal*, *Gabrielle d' Estrées*, and *Joseph*, all from 1806/07—shows the use of the abbreviation "b" for bassoons, whereas "fag" is characteristic of later manuscripts. (I am grateful to M. Elizabeth C. Bartlet and to Jean-Michel Nectoux of the Bibliothèque Nationale for this information.)

A brief pencil sketch marked "Andante" is found on p. 22 under m. 282. It bears no clefs or key-signature but makes sense when read in B-flat major with its three staves in descending order allocated to violin, viola and bass. The time-signature is $\frac{2}{4}$. Since the writing is canonic and somewhat resembles mm. 16–18 of the finished Andante, it may well be a preparatory working for the second movement.

APPENDIXES

M2.R23834 v.6 Q
Mehul, Etienne-Nicolas,
1763-1817.
  Symphony no. 1 in G minor.

M2.R23834 v.6 Q
Mehul, Etienne-Nicolas,
1763-1817.
  Symphony no. 1 in G minor.